Tate's Mill

The Journey of a Traveling Heart

by

Gary L. Gruhl

Margaret & Joe -
Best friends forever,
Good reading
Gary L Gruhl

First published by AuthorHouse 04/05/04

ISBN: 1-4184-0279-6 (e-book)
ISBN: 1-4184-0280-X (Paperback)

This book is printed on acid free paper.

Printed in the United States of America
Bloomington, Indiana

When I am an Old Man and all I have to do

is walk through the memories of my past

I will also be able to walk through

my memories of Tate's Mill

Gary L. Gruhl

Summer 1995

I found out something yesterday. If you're angry or upset
with someone
or you got this feeling of bitterness toward someone
you feel like you wanta hurt someone
        you can't get to Tate's Mill!

You can't get there from here!
        Or better -
                You can't get here from there!
I tried!
        I couldn't find it!
It was gone.
        And I knew
                that I knew the way!

And the harder I tried, the more I knew I could never find
 it. Until I dealt with what it was that was bothering me
and making me angry.

And then, after I had dealt with it and discarded it then -
        finally-

                I made it to Tate's Mill!

I found an old friend today. Just happened across it. It's called Tate's Mill. If you draw a line southwest and on either side of that line - going out about 8 or 10 miles - the whole country's like this.

It's a place where the bluffs run. The fields are - not terraced but contoured the way they should be. A strip of grain, a strip of alfalfa, a strip of corn. And you can smell the grain, and the corn and the alfalfa.

The sweetness of it all! Absolutely, marvelously restful place. The farms are clean - well kept up. Farmers working in the field always have a wave for the person driving by. And always a hand out in welcome.

The place that each of us wants to go in our heart. No one makes a judgment on us. Or on the mistakes that we make. We are welcome just because of WHO we are. And because of those mistakes. Because it makes us unique and different. Wonderful and exciting!

Tate's Mill is a place that anyone can go. Maybe everyone has their own Tate's Mill. All I have to do is close my eyes and I can be there. Or I just let my mind go there. And I can see the grain waving in the breeze. And the corn bursting out, filling the corn cribs.

I met a couple of children from Tate's Mill. Two sisters, Emily and Sara, aged 5 and 9. They had a brother who was 13 but he was a brother and didn't count for much in their lives at this moment. The thing I remember most was the joy that these two found in each other. All it took was a look from one to the other and they would break out in giggles. What a unique pleasure they shared with me that day.

There was this cloud over Tate's Mill today. Looked kinda like the way they used to depict jets in cartoons in the 40's. Large fat body, small sharp wings. Kinda like it was just cruisin' by making sure everything was okay.

The colts are running in the fields of Tate's Mill. A colt, the young cattle, and the people. Unbelievable!

And the season is whatever you want it to be. A mystical place that everyone searches for, but seldom finds. Because they are too busy. Or they are searching too hard.

I saw some boys from Tate's Mill playing volleyball today. What exuberance! What joy in just being alive. They didn't even bother to keep score. Their laughter and joy in living is like an elixir, giving new life and strength.

The sun always shines in Tate's Mill. Except, of course, if one wants the rain to fall warm upon their face. That also happens. But we keep the sun here even then.

Along the roads of Tate's Mill, there are an unbelievable number of yellow flowers. Poking their heads up and following the sun. Like a million little suns just welcoming you as you walk between the sides of the road. And both sides of the roadway have them. Like they want to share everything equally. They are prolific. And it's like they're dancing with the fairies in the breeze. What a wonderful place, this Tate's Mill!

Being lost is worth the coming home. It's no wonder the children wander to and fro. They must lose themselves to experience the warmth of coming home.

The children of Tate's Mill were running in the lea today. We don't have meadows here. We have leas. And it's strange - it's almost September and the wildflowers are still there - still up - still blooming! And the children are so full of joy and happiness. It's like they are little bottles of joy and they are just blowing the energy and joy out to the rest of the world. Their laughter is evident and you can hear it carried by the breeze. They are just full of the joy of living! And in Tate's Mill they still lie on their backs and watch the clouds skitter across the sky. Something that all of us have done and should do more often. But - we don't have the time.
We don't take the time.
We don't make the time!

Funny how Tate's Mill has always got the time. And it seems like still, everything gets done!

You know that in Tate's Mill every child has a pony. And the child in each of us has a horse. And we can ride those ponies and horses any time we want. Each of us also has a dog. And that dog is the perfect companion. Stays with us, never barks, always protective, always my friend.

And cats! It seems like cats belong to the community in Tate's Mill. They are all over. Brushing up against you. Crying for attention. And then, ignoring you when you reach down to pet them, like it's their due. Those cats!

Did you ever have one on those days when absolutely nothing went right? We don't have those days in Tate's Mill. Everything goes right here.

What a day it is. September! The breeze blowing. It is perfect, as it should be in Tate's Mill. The flag stands out straight from the flagpole, and there is a feeling, a touch of pride in your heart that it's your flag.

Tate's Mill. An ideal place to spend your time. Here in this little town of Tate's Mill, people going straight will stop to let you make a left turn. It's a - courtesy is a byword here. It's not something they do once in a while. It's a way of life.

And the train whistles. You can always hear the train whistles here. Calling you. But no one ever really goes.

And there's the machine shop. Almost like the old blacksmith shop.

What a place to live!

It's the kind of place you want to be from. And still want to live there. No, correct that! It's not the place you want to be from. It's the place you want to be!

There was a spot of gray that came into our sky today over Tate's Mill. But we just looked up at it and smiled. And it disappeared.. We're back to blue. Clouds are moving today.

In fact, they're performing a ballet for Tate's Mill. Just up there to make us happy.

Oh, and we have discovered the difference between solitude and loneliness is happiness. And so no one is ever lonely here in Tate's Mill. If someone wants to be alone, they can be alone. If they don't, they aren't. In Tate's Mill, we always have those with us that we want with us and those we love are always near.

Road wanderin'. Remember what it was like as a kid to stroll down the road at your own pace? Running when you wanted. Dragging your feet when you wanted. Raising dust if you wanted. That's the way it still is in Tate's Mill. Lots of us are out wanderin' the road. The road we are traveling here is happiness. In Tate's Mill, we find it. It is not a destination. When you make the happiness the road you are traveling - what a marvelous journey that makes for.

Road wanderin'. It's something you can do in Tate's Mill, that you can't do anywhere else. Because the speed is too great and the traffic is too heavy. But here in Tate's Mill, the road is wide and the tracks are dusty and you can do whatever you want down that road. And the dust devils dance.

Road wanderin'. What a time!
    With friends -
        With new found love.
Just walkin'. Wandering down the road. And the only place you're going is where you are. Nothing else exists. This point in time. This moment in time. This! This! What else needs to be.

Remember what it was like when you were young? And you went skinny dippin'? And you hit the edge of the lake or the swimming hole and you just stripped down. And then you hit the water? It didn't matter if you were boy or girl, male or female or black or white or Indian or Chicano. We were all the same. That's still the way it is in Tate's Mill. We didn't change. At any age you can still do that. And no one's going to look twice at you or stare at you when you strip down and run into the water. And you should run into the water when you are young. And we're all young here in Tate's Mill. But you better get ready to get wet. We are going to splash you or dunk you. We always have. We always will. If you come to the swimming hole, you are going to get wet.

And you're thinking that I live in a dream world. You're right! I do. That's where Tate's Mill is! Tate's Mill is a place where I don't have to worry about anything. When I'm in Tate's Mill, people accept me for what I am. Not for what they think I should be. Not for what I think I should be. But for what I am. And you and I are the same. We are one and equal. There is no difference between us.

The old swimming hole is just one of the many equalizers here in Tate's Mill.

Another of those equalizers is -
laying on the hill, watching clouds take different shapes. Today I've seen
        a witch,
        a tyrannosaurus Rex.

I've seen - no, that was yesterday I saw the jet plane. Today I see mountains. So many things up there. How many of these do we miss because we never look up? And we never take the time? How barren are your lives! Because you're afraid to stop and look up. Afraid someone will run you over! Or pass you by!

Take the time, my friend! It's worth it. Come visit me in Tate's Mill. Spend some time with me. You'll never want to leave. You can take a piece of it with you, and you never have to leave. You can come here anytime you like. No reservations needed. Always plenty of room. You want to come to Tate's Mill? Just close your eyes. Or - you don't have to close your eyes. Just think about us - think about you!

You ever seen a barn raisin'? You can see them at Tate's Mill. That's how we do most everything. Barn raisin's and garage raisin's and house raisin's. Whatever you want to be raised we do it here. It's just like a big party. It is a big party. We bring the whole place together. And we've always got the time to get this done. And we've always got time to help our neighbor. I wonder why that is? Maybe because we know that he's got the time to help us. Maybe because we know that time is the only element in our whole lives that once it's gone, we can never get it back! So we have to use it the best we can. And the best we can is to be happy. And the best we can is to help our neighbor. And the best we can is to help ourselves.

It always amazes me. We traded everything in the city for Tate's Mill and it was a good trade. And even for all we left behind, we are the better for it.

I just had something go completely out of my mind. Now in the city, they would look at me and shake their head in pity. Out here, they just think I'm quaint! I just love Tate's Mill! The gulls are out. Spiraling up today. Running back and forth in the sky. I wonder what that's about? What's going on? Why their excitement today? No one is plowing or tearing up ground. Maybe they are just happy. Maybe they just want to feel alive! And maybe they just enjoy flying. I wonder if I can get a piece of that sky? I can! I'm in Tate's Mill. Ah, I was wrong. Here's the farmer - and he is plowing - and the gulls are feasting. And there's the wave of the hand.

I love Tate's Mill!

Have you ever smelled the smell of buckwheat when it's blooming?
        Heard a baby cry?
You ever heard a lamb looking for it's mother?
        Or a little chick peepin' for its dinner?
Where have you spent your life?
You've missed the gems!
You've missed the jewels of life!

Did you ever see a flower as it opens? And in full bloom? You ever see a wolf as he's faced you down, and in his - not arrogance - but pride, just looked at you like, "Well, you poor son-of-a-gun!". Like we are actually the lesser creature. I ask you. Don't you just love the wolf? Look at those eyes! They could care less who you are.

Here in Tate's Mill, we're kind of at one with nature. It's like we and the earth are one. Hm. We are part of creation. We and the earth are one. I think it was Chief Joseph who said, "What happens to the earth, happens to each of us." Frightening thought! What happens to the earth happens to each of us. These are not the best of times then for the earth or for us.

Did you know that here at Tate's Mill everyone has a flag out? At least one! Some have four or five. We just love flags. We love to hear them snap in the wind. Did you ever listen to a large post flag snap in the breeze? There is nothing like that sound. Absolutely nothing like that sound.

And here in Tate's Mill there's not all the confusion about what is right and what is wrong. And who's got rights and who doesn't have rights. I mean, everybody's got the same rights. Who ever changed that? Who ever said they didn't? What have we become? Fools? What makes people think that there ever was a time when we didn't have those rights. We are all the same! I mean, when God made us, He didn't make one of us any less than the other. Or any more either! He made us all partners. And that's the way it should be. A relationship is built on love and respect. And that's the way it is in Tate's Mill. I think the biggest thing that we have going for us is respect for others. In Tate's Mill, there ain't no junk!!

A young man, a woman, they can hold hands and walk down the street. No one is going to laugh at them or ridicule them

or tease them. Oh, we might say, Hey, look at Susie and Jim!". But that's about as far as it goes. Nobody's gonna do anything to hurt anybody else around here. That's just not the way we do things here - -
In Tate's Mill.

You know in the big cities, you have to have addresses and all that stuff. Here in Tate's Mill, we don't need that. Cause everybody knows everybody else. And everything gets to everybody every day. Well. almost every day. You got something you want to get to Jim or Bob or Roy, give it to me, I'll get it there. Today or tomorrow. Or anyone else. They will get it there, too. And it don't have to get there today. Nothing ever does in Tate's Mill. And nothing runs in a straight line or even blocks around here. Out in Tate's Mill everything runs wherever God decided to put it down. And it seems to work just fine. I guess that's what happened when I traded that city for Tate's Mill. All those ideas, all that pressure, all that "Gotta do it now!" -
just went away. 'Cause out here in Tate's Mill, you don't have to do it now! In fact, no one is even gonna notice. And I can feel you laughing at me and thinking, "This guy is nuts!". There's no such place as Tate's Mill. But you're wrong!!
I've been there. And you've been there, too. You hate to admit it. - That you liked it. And you would like to go back there. But you're afraid. You're afraid somebody will walk by you, get one step up on you on the ladder.

Does it matter? At the end of time - is it going to matter? Does what you do right now have any bearing on what is going to happen at the end of time? Are you any more than a speck of sand on a beach? Think about it! What's it worth? Is it worth the price? Can you take any of it with you?

And people always come back to Tate's Mill. They leave - but they always come back. And when they come back, they never leave again. 'Cause this is where they should be.

And all those things I used to have. Aches, pains, back trouble. Sleepless nights. They're not here. It's like I left them in the city. And here in Tate's Mill - they're just not here. They don't exist here. There is no pain. There are no sleepless nights. The place where you want to be. This is the place where you should be. This is the place that each of us searches for in our hearts. The place we yearn for all our lives and seldom find.

And we have this little tiny church here in Tate's Mill. You'd love it. So friendly. And you know
how some churches say they are non-denominational. Not us! We are all-denominational. You can come in here no matter what you are. You're welcome. Come on in!

If you want to see the rain, you have to get up early, cause it don't rain in the daytime here. Unless someone wants to walk in the rain. Most of the time it will only rain at night. You'll see evidence of it in the morning - dripping off the houses and the trees. The sky will be clear and you won't see the rain. What a wonderful place to live!

Riding the horse today. Those gusty fall winds. Certainly will take your hat off if you're not careful. Almost took you off the horse if you weren't paying attention. What a wonderful day for riding.

To try and find specific words that would describe this place. I'm not sure but as I was thinking - the phrase the pastures of heaven came to mind. This is the place of dreams. This is the place where every dream is happening. And every dream is real.. Every hope that we have will come to fruition. This is where all of your dreams turn to wishes and all of your wishes come true. This is the place you thought about. This is the place you'd like to be! The place you want to be. The place you should be. This is the place you have to be! If you don't come here, you've never been anywhere. And once you've been here, you'll always come back.

There's a grove of trees here. Those trees look like they were planted when Moses was a baby.. Isn't it wonderful to be here? And each one is different and balanced in it's own way. It's evident that the Master Pruner was at work here! Only God can make a tree. And I don't think it was any quirk of fate that His only Son was a carpenter. Someone who works with his hands. Someone who knows that the wood can almost come alive when it's worked.

Come home. Come home to Tate's Mill!

There is this only tree that stands out.

All alone - like a prairie sentinel.

How did it get it's start? Who allowed it to grow? Why? In the middle of a field where everything else is tilled every year, what touched that farmer's heart to let this living example of God's handiwork spring up in the middle of his field?

Comin' Home

There are no goodbyes in Tate's Mill. No one stands at the railroad station and cries. Or gazes longingly at the bus station - and cries.

Those things don't happen here!

What we have is the comin' home. The joyous smiles at the station - when they see someone step off - that they haven't seen for a long time.

Or at the bus station. To catch their face -- in the window of the bus, as the bus pulls in.

What are the lonely places to most towns -
are places of joy and happiness in Tate's Mill.
Because that's a place of homecoming.

And even if people do get on those buses and those trains - and move away from Tate's Mill-

That, too, is part of the homecoming. Because you have to be away, to have the comin' home.

That is the joy!

Maybe not the same kind as when they step off the train
and we can touch them
and hold them again.

But, it's the kind that knows they have to take that step to grow,
and become who they're gonna be.

This thing about somebody leaving and somebody always left behind. That's not the way it has to be. Although that's the way most people think it has to be.

We stay with those that leave!
     And those that leave come home.
          There is no goodbye!

We too often allow time to become our enemy
     instead of our friend.
We don't take the time to do those things we should do.
     A time to sit on top of a hill
          gaze across fields
          rich with harvest or with promise.
     Or to sit on top of bluffs
          looking across the entire expanse
               of the river bottom.
     And just sit there and enjoy -
          there is no other way to describe it
               - the hand of the Creator.

What are we afraid of?
Why do we run swiftly from this-
               this beauty?
Why do we put ourselves in this mold of trying to acquire things?
     Things that really have no real value.

I think that one of the things we miss the most but don't realize it is the strain of muscle under the skin. I remember it. I guess not the strain, but the workings, the rhythm of it.

15

How good it felt. With the sun beating down! Grain to be moved. Bales of hay to be thrown.

How good it felt at the end of the day to have accomplished that kind of work, and to know what you had finished.

Comin' Home

It's been one of those short periods when I had to leave
Tate's Mill, and today -
I have the opportunity to come back home.
To where it began,
      where it continues,
           where it will end.

It's a good feeling to know that all of life has a continuity
- and -
      even though it seems like it's a small, tiny place in
actual fact, it's not! 'Cause the feelings that come over me
      when I think of this place,
      when I see certain things

Nothing can contain those feelings-
      those feelings are larger than life itself.
 Larger than anything most
      people have experienced.

Have you ever felt the comin' home?
Do you know what it's like comin' home?
The joyous feeling that - I'm not sure
      nothing seems to match it

nothing seems to explain it
nothing seems to -
It's just such a
                    feeling
        not a feeling -
a powerful   -   something
It seems to just fill you up with -
        I don't know...
Is it the security?
Is it the warmth?
Is it the absolute accceptance?
What is it you get from the comin' home?

All the time I was growing up, and bringing friends over.
It was like when I crossed the door - everything fell away.
When I was going to school, it was the same. There was no
pretense or anything like that. When you came through the
door, you were you and that's why you were here and that's
why you were accepted.
That's kinda like this whole thing at Tate's Mill.

It's just - -
        just one big family.
And when you come home -
        we know that you're here for safety
                and warmth
                        and comfort
    and friendship, and all those thing that you're running to
- they're here!
And all those things you've been running from - they're not
here.
        We don't let them in.

And you don't have to bring them in with you.
Leave them outside!

Drop them at the gate. Everything, - <u>everything</u>, stays outside.
The only things that come in here are those things we want to bring in with us.

There's a sign up outside of Tate's Mill. It's - - just a handwritten sign as you're coming in. Not sure who even did it, but it's fairly evident and you can't miss it. Just got two words on it. It just says simply "Welcome Home". And you come by that so often that you never really think about what it says. But just to have that
"Welcome Home!"
To have a place where you are welcome. To have a place that is home.

How often we forget what is precious to us.
How often we take for granted those things that are beyond value.

"Welcome Home".

A large part of what we are is memories.

And sometimes we try to color those memories to fit what we would like them to be. Why don't we do it right the first time? And make these times   - that make memories - exactly what we want them to be?

What are we afraid of?

In any relationship -
> if we are going to get anything out of it-

We have to be ready to take the risk of some pain.
> But even pain is part of the relationship.

Here at Tate's Mill, it even happens to us sometimes. But it's like - it's like the leaving. You know! If you want to come home, you first have to leave. If you want love, you have to experience some of the cement that's going to hold it together. And while love builds on the good times - what holds love together is being there through the bad times. And knowing that love is there - no matter what.
Kind of like the love that God has for us.
You know - it's always there!
And in these relationships, we sometimes fail to recognize that, or maybe we're afraid to recognize it.
If we know someone loves us -
> that's a scary proposition sometimes.

And again, we're thinking of what it's going to cost me.

Why can't we look at it from the flip side? 'Cause it's not going to cost you anything. Love in a relationship can only make your life more fruitful and enjoyable. And yes, there are risks involved. Because when we fall in love, or we develop a friendship that's deep and intense - we're not gonna be the same as we were before! We're gonna change. We are not going to be who we are now!

And all of us fear change. But maybe we should - -
> just maybe - - we should look forward to the change.

Sometimes we as the "educated" people in the world think that we've got wisdom also. I think that the wisdom has been here forever. All we gotta do is find it.

I ran across a Swahili chant that says:

Life has meaning only in the struggle.
Triumph and defeat are in the hands of the gods.
So let us celebrate in the struggle!

"Celebrate in the struggle"
Everything is a joy.
		So let's go through it together.

And doing it
		our joy will be multiplied.

Anything shared always gets better.

THE MILL

You know the old saying about the grass is always greener on the other side of the fence?

Well, not here in Tate's Mill!

For two reasons. Number one - the grass is always green. And secondly, we don't have fences.

People ask about Tate's Mill.
Where's the mill?
Who was Tate?

No one knows for sure.

There is a story about a young couple.
About how a young couple came out here -
     madly in love.
A miller - and his bride.
And they built the mill.
And this was where they were going to be.
And the story says that you never saw two happier people.

It was said that he told her, because of their love, he had seen more through her in an instant than all men had seen for all eternity. Gives you some idea of how much they cared for one another.

Then some illness took the young man's bride. Took his joy away. And nothing could comfort him. They say he cried for days.

And then -

one day - he stopped crying.

And he went up to the mill that he and his wife had built. And he took it apart.

It wasn't like we normally would take something down. Where we would actually demolish it. Where the goal is just to get it down and as quickly as possible.

They say he tenderly took this mill apart. Piece by piece. Stacked the wood they had used. Moved the stone back to the quarry. And all the time he was doing this, they say he never spoke a word to anyone.

And when the mill was completely down, he packed up their belongings in a wagon and disappeared to the west. It was said that just before he went over the ridge where the view would be cut off, he stopped and looked back one last time.

That's the story of the mill. No one's ever found the foundation. There have been stones that have been cut before found in the quarry from time to time. No one knows who cut 'em. And if you look closely, you can see signs of mortar on those stones.

Still we wonder - where's the mill?

Oh, the children keep searching along the river and from time to time they find a flat place -
    or a -
        something that looks like it might be a possibility.
Then, of course,

they come home and tell their folks, and their folks pick up their excitement, and the next thing you know, we kinda get a party together
> - and we go out there.

And we snoop around -
> and finally come to the conclusion that

No - this wasn't where the mill was.

We know there was one! What we don't know is where. At least there is one part of the mystery that we do know.

There's an old faded photograph with a picture of the mill and this handsome couple -
> beautiful lady -
>> standing in front of it.

Tate's Mill written across the front of the picture. Ink so faded we can just barely make it out.

But it was taken fairly close up to the mill. So we can't find the place on the river where it might have been taken. At least not from landmarks.

I wonder -
> sometimes-

I wonder why he found it necessary to dismantle the mill.
Was it that all his dreams
> were tied up in the mill?

I wonder.
Could his other dreams break free only after it was released from the mill? Could it have been done any other way?

No. Not for Tate.

We never had another mill.

But somehow, the name took hold.

He took part of his dream with him in the wagon,
        but a part of it stayed here for us.

Old Jim. He tries to stay on top of these various sightings and so forth that we come upon and investigate. He has this old plat map -
and each position that we've looked over and agreed upon is marked upon his map. With notes - and possibilities.

I guess Jim uses it as something to keep him busy. Funny thing is - Jim says he remembers the mill - but... He can't quite remember where it was. It's one of those things all of us have. Kinda sittin' there! Jim goes out and he says he knows in his mind that if he ever sees the place, he'll know it. And it's kind of like a little piece of his past that's lost - and he's trying hard to remember it.

He remembers that old photograph. He -
He says that's the mill and that's the way it looked.
But he can't place it in his mind. And he was just - I don't know - no one really knows how old Jim is anyway. He doesn't himself! He says he was just a pup when Tate took the mill down. But he keeps trying to find that little piece of his past. One little piece he thinks will bring it all together.

I think that's part of Jim's dream. He's got that something to search for. And he keeps on looking. He finds joy in the search!

And the times that he's looked. And the adventures he's had. Just trying to find that mill.

And you're thinking - "You all are fools! You say you can't find the mill. If you really wanted to find it, you'd set up a sweep and move up and down the river until it came to be". But -
> that would take the joy out of it.

Part of the joy of being here is that <u>maybe</u> we'll find it someday.

A lot of the joy of living here is <u>not</u> finding it!

Because you've always got something to look forward to. Think about that! You've <u>always</u> got something to look forward to.

Can you say that about any other part of your life?

Something to look forward to with excitement,

> happiness,

> anticipation!

The kind of things like -
> like kids looking forward to Christmas.

It's that kind of looking forward.

Makes us all human.
Holding on to hope.
Lookin' forward.

Being lost is worth the comin' home!

THE BAND SHELL

In the band shell today, a solitary young man

no -
       wait.

       A young woman and her young man -

someone had moved a picnic table up into the band shell
       and-
both of them sitting,
          smiling -
          holding each other's hands.

And softly singing to each other -
Both unaware that their concert for each other was magnified
by the shell
and all of us who are sitting out front hear,
          and share their feelings.

Or perhaps -
       they are aware
          and wanted to share it with us.

Youth - -
       And love –

       Oh, that we could always hold that joy!

FOGGY BOTTOMS

There's fog over the bottoms of Tate's Mill today. Kinda nice.

You just -
one second you're there - the next second you're not. Kinda like you're operating in a world all your own.

If you're looking for solitude - this is the day for it. Everyone's in solitude today. They go fifteen feet away from you - you can't even see them. The fog's so thick you can cut it with a knife. If you walk through it, it's like you are walking through light water.

It's a wonderful day!

Foggy bottom. That's really where we are. And a lot of people call us that, too.

Now that was something I had never seen before. We're standing here in the midst of this fog. And it's so thick you almost have to cut it -
and all of a sudden you see a slice of lightning coming through it. This Tate's Mill - always full of surprises. Every day we see more and more.

What a place - this Tate's Mill. The fog's so thick - you would think the clouds were walking. And it's that kinda day, too. If the clouds want to walk - what do you want to do? Man - we want to sit in front of a fire and watch the fire dance! Can't even see the top of the bluffs. It's like you look up - and you see a couple of trees and a house - and then - all of a sudden the bluff just disappears into the fog. It's like the hand of God is sitting over everything - keeping it quiet - holding it close!

What a beautiful smile! It's amazing somehow, at times just what a smile can be - what a smile can do. I mean your day can be crummy and things can be going ---

Ah, but excuse me! Not here in Tate's Mill. Your day can't be going like that.

But your day can be going - not quite right. All of a sudden, you see this smile. And it becomes a unique experience. Isn't it amazing what a smile can do??

THE CHILDREN

There was a mist over Tate's Mill this morning. The kind where - when you walk the water will gather on your face and run down your cheeks.

Now some folks would consider this a real nuisance, but here in Tate's Mill, it is a matter of joy.

You see kids running through the mist. Sticking their tongues out, trying to catch the water as it runs down their faces.

These are the times we should live for! These little bits of happiness - that are all around us. Always here!

Most often folks would shout at their children and tell them to grow up. Heaven forbid!

Let's let our children be children.

Let's revel in the joy that they find. If we can hold onto our children's joy or the joy that we found as children in the simple things - we'd find that all of our "problems" would disappear overnight.

When we were kids and we asked for something and they said "no" - we just kinda shrugged our shoulders and said "okay" and moved on.

As we grew older, we lost the capability to move on. Now we have hurt feelings - and try to justify why we should have gotten what we didn't get.

Instead of just saying "okay" and shrugging our shoulders and moving on.

How much simpler our lives would be.

Yes, they would be -...

Saw a girl on the playground this morning. Others were playing some kind of kick ball.

And she was watching them. She was playing, too - she was watching the person with the ball -
while she was waiting, she was going through these intricate ballet steps out there.

It was just the most wonderful thing to watch. - She was, well - she was in our world but she was in a world of her own also. There was delight in her movement. There is no other way to describe it. She was just a pure point of gladness. And she found joy in the movement. In the stirring of her moment in time.

What joy children hold in their hearts and exhibit in their actions. How uninhibited they are. How blessed in their freedom. And for most of them - they do not even realize how much fun they are having - or perhaps they do.

Or how much joy they are bringing to others. They are unaware of the power of their happiness.

And aren't we all? - Unaware of the power of our happiness!

I saw a Mom today, and she was working in the yard. Her little girl had been out helping her. And the little girl just wandered away and hid behind a short section of fence.

Mom came back - came walking toward her little girl. This little girl stepped out from behind that section of fence - and her Mom said,"Hi!" - but the expression of joy on that mother's face when she saw her little girl was beyond description.

Her face - the smile on the face of that little girl - how it lit up when she saw her Mom. And when her Mom's face lit up to her.

It was like two suns shining on each other.

What a place -
this Tate's Mill!

DAY AND NIGHT

Clouds.

Now I know you'll find this hard to believe, but - we had a cloud cover over Tate's Mill today.

But, - I think it was just so we could have this afternoon.

It was kind of a cool day. Nothin' nasty or anything like that --

>   it was a nice day -
>   overcast

but not gloomy.

But now getting close to sundown -
I tell you
>   it is absolutely -

Astounding!

The cloud cover moving to the east. And the sun going down in the west. And that sky is so bright over there -
I tell you -
it looks like somebody's got the high place on fire.

This Tate's Mill.

What a place to be!
It happened today. Two people walking down the street toward each other. One about 16 - head down, hunched over, studying the ground as she walked. The other about 40 - called out to the younger and smiled and spoke. The

younger, now head up, back straight, smile on her face, eyes sparkling. Only a few words passed between them. Smiles exchanged. What a lovely miracle.

The power of a smile.

A fine day here in Tate's Mill. The clouds are racing across the sky. Just tiny little puffers -
but they are racing so fast, it looks like they got appointments somewhere.

Remember what it was like to sleep in the sun? To find that place where the wind couldn't get to you,
but the sun could!
You'd just lay on your back
or your stomach
and let the sun just bake you.
Especially on those cool fall days when it was almost uncomfortable to to be out, but if you were where the sun was shining and the wind couldn't find you -
there was - -
there are no words to properly describe it.
Just the warmth,
and the sleeping,
and the safety.

There was a full moon over Tate's Mill this morning. It's like all of a sudden, the night was calling.   It was about 3:00 a.m..

I went out -
there it was -- full in the sky.

It was like, well -
it was like being under a white sun.

Saw the morning star this morning, too. Absolutely brilliant,
clear morning. And leading up to that from the earth - a
rainbow sunrise.
What a marvelous hand has the Creator. If only we open our
eyes to see.
I think what makes me feel so good about this
       Tate's Mill -
I think it's the,
it's kinda like when you fall in love.

It's like you and the one you're falling in love with - your
hearts beat at the same time,
       you follow in the same rhythm.

That's kinda what it's like here in Tate's Mill. We are all
kinda in the same rhythm. We're all the same one.

It's kinda hard to explain -
       but it's

It's not a singleness of purpose -
       that's not it.
More like a singleness of hope!

It's like the joy that we have when we come here is multiplied
because others are here for some of the same reasons.

And you can see that joy,
       and feel that joy,

and hear that joy!!
It's in their eyes and their smiles -
And -
not only are they willing - but they want to share.
It's almost like it's a necessity,
but it's not -

You know -
it's like a want,
not a need - wanting to share that joy.

It's like we know that joy - not joy but -
like love isn't love till it's given away.
You can't have love and joy and keep it all to yourself.
It has to be shared to be truly experienced.
Remember when you were a kid how, if you went into some kind of little trance - just daydreaming - People would always snap you out of it?
Tell you to "Stop daydreaming!".

Well, that's not the way it is here in Tate's Mill.

Here in Tate's Mill, we never want you to stop dreaming.

In this place, our life is our dreams.
And if you can dream it, it can happen.

It's a place where each of us can take that segment of our heart -
and play it over -
and <u>know</u> that whoever happens upon it is going to treat it with love and respect. No one's going to snap you back and

41

say "Stop dreamin'!". Here in Tate's Mill, we try to share our dreams. Most of us tend to do that anyway.

> A greeting on the street, or
> a wave of the hand.
> Just a smile sometimes.

That's all it takes to enfold each of us in the dreams of others. We may not know the specifics of everything that's happening -
but we know for that one brief instant, we were included in their dream.
That we were a part of their joy and happiness,

> And they -
>> were a part of ours!

Dreams are the things life is made of. And outside of Tate's Mill, it seems like for the most part, it's all turned around.
Outside, we don't even like to think about dreams, because they seem to be unattainable or unrealistic.

Here in Tate's Mill, our dreams are our reality.
Or rather, reality is our dreams!
Everything we look for

> and hope for
>> and wish for

Everything we want for our children, our family, friends, grandchildren - it's all here.

All you gotta do is come home!
Another thing that seems to be our enemy that should be our friend is Time.

Outside of Tate's Mill, it seems like we keep getting trapped in those same time boxes. Where everyone's got a deadline they gotta meet.

The only deadline that exists in Tate's Mill is the one you put on yourself.

Once you've been here
And once you've found us.
You find that there aren't any limits at all.

Time is our friend here. We don't have to <u>make</u> the time or <u>take</u> the time to do things here. Time comes to us.
'Cause all the things that seem important outside of Tate's Mill are not important here.
Big house, fancy car, expensive clothes -
Forget that!

All that we look for here is an open home,
        a warm hearth!
Someplace to put our feet up with friends,
        on a winters day.
A table to sit around -
        coffee, hot cider.
Just enjoying our friends, being with them.

We hardly take that time anymore outside of Tate's Mill.

You want to get it back?
You really want to find it?

Have you had it before, and you would really like to get it back?

Come visit me in Tate's Mill!

It's not that hard to do. You know people you would like to do this with!
Make it happen - Dream your dream.
Only you can make that dream come true!

THE DAWN

There is nothing like the sky at dawn. That - that color - no
matter what particular color it happens to be, it's always just
-

                     beautiful.

And up the cloud bank -
the clouds have a wonder all their own.
This morning, just a few,
               sporadic, little clouds over the dawn.
It's like they are brighter light - like they're - I don't know
- like beacons of hope.

It's sort of a joyous feeling just to see it.

The sunrise again this morning -
      it's -
              I guess it's not so surprising -
      'cause each one is different!

This morning was a special treat. Was up early enough so
that all the stars had disappeared -
      with the exception of the morning star.
And as you looked to the dawn -
      there were fingers of light reaching up -
      and
      I don't know how to describe the colors -
it's not red -
             it's not yellow -
                       it's not orange -
It's just beautiful!
But it was like there were fingers -
      reaching out from the dawn -

up to the morning star.

I just watched in amazement.
    I -
        words cannot describe it.

Can you see it? I hope you can. I want to share it with you.
It is too much to keep to myself.
I love this time, long before dawn. When the dark is still
dark and the stars are so bright in the sky. Like every one
is a -
        just up there twinkling.
And the moon casting it's glow across the land.
And the quiet!
What you hear is the sound of yourself. And the other
sounds you can identify.
The lone dog barks - once! Just to let you know, he knows
you are out.

Had a real nice rain last night. Thunderstorms. Lightning.
Heavy rain.

This morning dawned clear and bright. And the thing that
got me most was - I took this morning to stop, and climb the
bluff overlooking Farr's Creek.

It's like the creek was singing a song this morning. On this
particular spot, there is a -
I wouldn't call it rough water right below but, it's like a
gentle rapids. The creek running over rocks. With the creek
being up and the water making a good run -
        the melody is just -

music for the soul.
You felt you could have stayed there all day and just listened.
One of those sweet sounds that you are blessed with.

Got the fog rising off the bottoms today.
And the sun - a bright red-orange coming up over the bluffs.
And the land is so green! If I didn't know better, I would think I was in heaven.

It's the kinda morning one can lose oneself in. This is the kind of morning you should be on the bottoms, waiting for the sun to burn off the fog. Watching it slowly as it lifts.

If you asked me what was right with it, I would be hard pressed to give you specific ideas on exactly what it is.

But suffice it to say - There isn't anything wrong with this morning. And as I stand here, on the top of the bluff now, and take a slow turn at the picture that is spread out before me - I cannot begin to tell you how wonderful it is.
And then, the cuts and switch backs here that run down from the bluff.
The trees form a canopy over the earth. And you can't see what's going on down there. But you know there's so much activity, so much going on.
You can feel it, even if you can't see it!

And we wish we could be a part of it.
But we can't!
'Cause we've always got our priorities set in the wrong place.

There are so many different shades of green out here this morning that you can't count them.

And the earth has a softness to it today.

The sky is clear. Just a few, wispy clouds.
All is at peace out here.

I wonder what would happen on days like this if no one went to work. And everyone just took the opportunity to take some pleasure in the sheer majesty of nature. I dare say that, in the long run, people would be a lot happier. And in the long run, everybody would probably make a lot more money. Because a happy employee produces a lot better than one that's not.

And sometimes, just the smallest things can bring pleasure when we're not expecting them.

Like - the cry of the kildeer can take you back to those times when you were young and growing up. When we used to tease them by coming by and the mother would pretend her wing was broken and try to lead us away from the nest. But we would just ignore her. And then, once we found the nest, we made sure we never came back close to it again. Just kids.

These are the days we look forward to. Coming to the end of summer. Cool. Sunny. Every day makes you glad you are alive. The clouds just sit there in the sky. Daring you to lay on your back and watch them. And they move ponderously today.

They're not in any hurry.
    So why should we be?

And as you run between the bluffs today, the trees seem to take on a deeper shade of green.
Except one or two -
    just random
    who have taken on their autumn colors.
The deep red -
    the brilliant orange -
        the shocking yellow.
These are the times and the scenes that make the soul sing. These are the times that make life worth living. These are the little snippets that we have to hold onto when nothing else seems to be going right. We have to take these little pieces of Tate's Mill and keep them in our minds eye and never let them go.

Another cool, fall morning!
These are the days of the gathering. When the fruit of the harvest is ready. And everyone is bringing it in.

And not only us!

But all of the creatures of the forest are gathering. The squirrels, the chipmunk. Taking in the fruit of the earth. And putting it away for the time ahead.

A quiet morning. The lakes are like glass. Like giant mirrors reflecting the sky and shoreline.

What a marvelous thing is the hand of this Creator. And what a marvelous thing is the gift that allows us to see and hear and appreciate this creation.

FALL

You should have seen the moon over Tate's Mill this morning.

I was out a little earlier -

just a bit of a cloud cover, but you could see the stars. And there's that hook of a moon just sitting there in the sky -

smiling down at you.

It's easy to see why ancient man perhaps worshipped the moon -

it is a thing of wonder -

And as bright as it is, how it changes.
Not having the capability to find out why those changes were - just to see the change -
and wondering -
and now, knowing all those things, it's still a - just a positive wonder. And an object of beauty.

The colors are starting to turn on the bluffs. It is hard to imagine that there can be that many different shades and colors. What a marvelous hand this Creator has. What a Master's touch for color.

I wonder what it is about fall days. If it was this temperature in the height of summer, we would all be freezing -

but here in the fall -

It's like a tonic!

And -

It's just -

It's full of -
I guess full of life is the only way to describe it. It's a buoyant feeling. Like you're on top of the world. The breeze hits you and it's got - maybe - just a touch of cold in it. But doesn't it feel <u>good</u>!

It feels cool,
    and welcoming,
        and wonderful!

And it's like that all over.

This time of year -
    the cold mornings -
        the warm afternoons.
Saw the children out playing today and in one corner of the playground -
    a mound of jackets and coats.
Just right for this morning but far too much for the afternoon!!

What happens to us as we grow older? There is no way we would do that! Throw our coat in the corner of the playground and join in on joy and happiness. Would that we could hold onto it forever.
Explosions of color. No other way to describe it. An absolute explosion!!

It's kinda late in the year now. A lot of the green is gone. We now have the amber and gold of harvest.

But the creeks are still running -
>and
>>down in the hollows -
>the trees are still holding their leaves.

On the top of the bluffs the trees look like black skeletons
facing the sky,
>then every once in awhile,
>you come upon a tree that
>>just doesn't seem to understand that the
season is over.
It's standing there -
>green -
>>full.

What a place! This Tate's Mill.

Harvest time in Tate's Mill.
Beans are ripe. Corn is ripe.

It is absolutely amazing - the bounty that comes out of the
earth.

And there's a restlessness -
and I hardly know where it is coming from.

If it was spring, I could call it spring fever. But it's fall.
Nothing seems to satisfy. Seem tired all the time, but sleep
doesn't seem to help or take care of it. Like your body was
searching for something,
>but you have no idea what!

Even at this stage, the smell of new-mown hay -
The difference in the fall is - it doesn't seem quite as - I'm
not sure what it is. It's a little drier, a little sweeter -

My Dad always used to say that the third cutting was the best
- and if you could get that fourth cutting - that was better yet.
So fine!

Always good chewing on a stem.

It's like it's finally fall. Like the leaves are celebrating the
end of summer. Throwing their leaves like confetti in the
air. They're coming down. The leaves are coming down in
droves and
      covering the ground
          in a blanket of color.
I mean, the ground is like -
      a quilt done in patchwork -
          with small irregular patches.

And sometimes between these little bluffs where the farms
have been set in for years, there's a series of little holding
ponds that somehow got placed in the exact right position.

There is this one in particular that is just marvelous. It's
spring fed, the top one and there are two more below it.
There is no way though, that you could have three of these
ponds in a row like that. I know that at some time they were
built up on purpose. But over the years, it's become part of
the land.
And it looks like -
      that's the way it is -

And -

      the kids have discovered these pools. And they're deep and clear and
you've never seen joy and exuberance
      and just the thrill of being alive -
            until you've watched these kids romping through a series of
            holding ponds.
      that are clear,
         and cold,
            and inviting.
In the fall, it is interesting to notice even in the small bluffs, the cattle will lay on the lee side of the bluff and take their moment in the sun.

And the houses and so forth that were put here with such care. They too protect themselves. They are on the lee side or are set into the lee side.

What a marvelous country -
      this Tate's Mill!
      Varied,
            beautiful!
Well, there certainly was frost on the pumpkin this morning at Tate's Mill. And if you had those water buckets out and full, there'll be a real light layer of ice across the top of the bucket.

I love this time of year, when everything is ripening down. And you can see what the writer meant when he said "amber waves of grain".

This is the promise that spring gave to us. And we can see it now! And the smell of the last cutting of hay. This is truly what each promise of spring brings us. And when we live to see the fruits of these promises.

It's kinda like watching your children grow. When they're born, you see all the possibility and promise.
In the fall of the year. Another one of those feeling you get sometimes is - you'd like to just slip onto a boat and slip away. You would like to run the river one last time. And maybe stay where the climate is gonna be warm for the winter.

There fantasies we all hold onto. These dreams we never quite put into action. These dreams are the things that keep us going. Help us look forward to -
 tomorrow - and beyond.

Getting into the time where it seems like it can nip at your nose. Wonderful day. Starts at about 25 degrees - going to get up to about 65 before it is over.

These are the days that make you glad you are alive. These are the days of hope. Seems like the day starts out cold and ends up warm - kinda like we want our relationships to be.

Don't you love to watch what the wind does to trees. How it makes them dance and sway. How each tree does it's dance a little bit different.
What a variety of places - scenes -
How much do you look for?
 Who do you look for anymore?

How much do you really see?

Some other signs are evident. The birds are tending to flock. Do you see them? You can see them, gathering in ever increasing numbers - feeding - for that long journey that's ahead of them.

And the geese and the ducks in those V's of ever increasing length. Can't you see them?
Moving back and forth across the sky - seemingly in wait for that inevitable day when - instinct will turn them south - and they'll move on for the winter.

What a glorious vista is this Tate's Mill. To stand on top of the bluffs and look to the North - Look to the South. There are certain points on the bluff where you can see for miles and miles and miles! And you have to work to get to those points, but the view is well worth it.
You can stand up there and look -
and see more beauty and grace in five minutes,
than most people ever see in their whole lives.

You can move your eyes a couple of inches - the whole vista changes. You have a whole new picture. You're gonna see more of life in a half-hour than you can see anywhere else on the planet!

You can see a farmer with his kids working and making play out of work and doing it together.
You can see deer with their yearling fawns.

The rabbits moving hesitantly across each clear patch.

What an amazing place - this Tate's Mill.

I always love dropping down into the cuts - between the bluffs.
Whether it's in a vehicle or on horseback - sometimes just runnin' down the sides of the bluff (although as age comes on the running is more like a quick amble). Especially at this time of year. The further you come down, the longer delayed the fall is. And you can still find the green and the lushness here.

It sits right alongside the gold of harvest!
Marvelous place, this Tate's Mill.

The possibilities of what you can do here are beyond what you can imagine. Because you can do here, anything you want to do. Think of it! This is your place! Not anyone else's!

The smell of wood smoke and burning leaves.
What visions do these smells provoke?

The stars were being blown about this morning by a warm wind. Following a black night. A prelude to the white of winter? It's still the type of night you should be out and a bonfire should be blazing. A light in the midst of the darkness.

The leaves are starting to turn.
It seems like once -

one tree starts to change - it's like all the rest are trying to keep up. They all want to make sure no one gets ahead of anyone else.

The riot of color just continues to increase.

It's a kind of picture postcard morning. As you look to the east, the sky is blue. And it's got this band of color -
Even to try and describe the colors would be a disservice.
It's such a beautiful mix.

Before the sun comes up - the sun has colored the entire horizon and painted a pleasure for the eyes. And as you look through that, you can still catch the stars. And they are just brilliant.

And the fog in the bottoms this morning is -
    well -
    if you were walking through it, you would need a handkerchief to wipe the water off your face. That's how heavy the fog is this morning.
And the smell in the air is that of -
    just such a tremendous lushness.
Like all the bounty of the earth is putting it's essence into that smell!

THE HOLLOW

There's this place in Tate's Mill called "the Hollow". And if you're driving by on the road,
it's - well, you can't even see it, or even know it's there. Daytime or nighttime, it's exactly the same! If you don't know it, it's not there! Just one of those things that's passed from parent to child - parent to child.

This is one of those places where - - you really can get away from it all. Everything here is - well, it's hard to describe. As you come off the main road, heading south, you head down this little dirt track and all of a sudden, it turns to the left and starts to take you down. And then, just as suddenly, it bottoms out.

It's almost like somebody planned it out - there's a place where you can park your car. Then you walk away from that - and your car disappears. You can't even see that.

And there's a flat place down there that sits right next to the creek. It's got places for one to two to fifty - How many people do you want? It's down there.

And the remnants of fires are there - from people burning them late at night. I remember some of those campfires. I remember looking up from those campfires and knowing there's two bodies on the blanket across the fire, but I only see one shape. And I know when they looked across at my blanket, it was kinda the same thing they were thinking.

I remember laying on my back on the grass. How cool the ground was. How bright the stars! How warm the fire!

It was just a place where you could be free.

This was part of what you did. Who you were. And we just didn't go down there to play kissy face, huggy bear. We went down there to be with our friends. There's nothing like it!

Campfires and - - You could run that fire up and nobody would ever know you're there. And the word would spread. It was like - one guy would say "the Hollow" and it would run like wildfire from one to the next - to the next. Before we knew it, we had a full blown gatherin' going on. Someone would always get there early and gather the wood, start the fire. By the time everyone else showed up with the food and the sodas, the sun was setting - the night was putting a little chill in the air - We all gathered around the fire. Sometimes told stories. Sometimes just laughed. Sometime just looked at each other - and had a good time.

Sometimes just an old songfest. Singing to our friends. No! Singing WITH our friends. Sometimes songs deep with longing. Sometimes songs full of joy. And sometimes songs just full of nonsense. But I guess most importantly,
        just songs with our friends.

Remember days like that?

There were a lot of things that happened down there by the creek. Down in the hollow. That creek ran through the property and there was a spring there that fed into the creek too. It wasn't the kind of spring you normally think of, where the water comes up in a nice, clear stream and you can see where it is - one that flows directly into the creek. This was a seepage spring. And I suppose the area that it covered was - oh, I don't know - 15 to 20 feet wide by 10 feet deep. And if you didn't know what this was - it looked terribly solid. Leaves had built up on it. It looked just like the floor of the rest of the hollow. And - - people would sometimes blunder across it. Only they wouldn't blunder more than two steps - 'cause that's all the further you could go into the spring, because by now, you are in up past your knees.

We had this one guy - he went in there - funniest thing we ever saw. He went in there - discovered what he was doing - when he got himself out of there, he had his shoes on - but his socks were missing. And he insisted that he had them all on when he went in. Never could explain that!

Strange things happen in the Hollow. Strange funny - not strange scary.

But I guess the nicest thing about the Hollow was that nobody expected anything of anybody. Everybody just kinda did what they wanted. Did their own thing! Didn't step on anybody else's toes. Didn't move into anybody else's territory. The Hollow was neutral ground. I guess we just kinda respected everybody else's space, you know? You have your space, I have mine. If my space comes into your space, I'm there because you want me there. And I want to be there.

I was in the heart of Tate's Mill today.
     The quiet -
          the peacefulness.

The majesty of this spot on God's earth.
I was out,
        just me and my dog.
And there was no one else as far as I could see.
And no sound -
        other than the sounds made by nature.
This is solitude at it's finest.
This moment.
Reveling in the music made by God!

There's a rooftop out here
        that you can see from the bluffs.
On the roof is painted,
        "Jesus is Lord"!

And not too far away -
a couple of homesteads that are empty now. And the only
thing left on them is the silos. And you know they're
homesteads because you can see the old groves on them that
were planted to protect the house and the outbuildings. But
-
  the silos just stand there now like -
        silent sentinels -
                guarding the memories of their homes.
Makes you wonder. What happened to those people? Did
the line just die out? What were their hopes and dreams?
They were here in Tate's Mill and -
        What happened?
        Where did they go?
Did their dreams come true?
Did they follow them somewhere else?
Did they come true for them there?

Was this abandoned homesite the end of their dream?
Or was it just the beginning?

RANDOM THOUGHTS

Looking to the east across the top of the bluff. The line of trees are silhouetted against the morning sky. The color is difficult to describe. It's not the color you think of when you think of sunrise. It's a brilliant hue - just the color of life!

And the Creator has taken and mixed that color with the blue above it - into a perfect blend, and then we run into the blue sky above it.

What a marvelous hand does this Creator have. What artistry. And what a way with color!

And the sun knifing through the pines -
sometimes just those single shafts of light, that somehow seem to be scattered in the middle of nowhere out here.

We have ribbons of steel that run out of Tate's Mill. Sometimes we can find the young men and women standing between those ribbons of steel - gazing down them. Those tracks seem to run endlessly - until you just loose sight of them.

I wonder, - are they just wondering what's out there?
What <u>are</u> they thinking?

Today, it's like a rain forest here in Tate's Mill. Not with the water dripping, but down here in the hollow the humidity just seems to hang - and it seems a lot warmer than it really is. It's a beautiful day for this time of year.

A construction project -

a huge mound of dirt -
and boys!

THE RIDGE

Last night we had a real show!

- As you look past Tate's Mill to the next set of bluffs -- had a lightning dance over there last night.

Once again, I am in awe at the hand of the Creator.

It was almost constant flashes.
   Out of a black sky.
A brilliant spear of light. Over - and over - and over. What a marvelous display!

Does He know the joy that we --
He must know the joy that we feel!
And now, when I think of that -
   if He feels the joy -
   then He must also share the sadness.

Is there a place your heart yearns for?
A place you've never been?
A place you can't quite describe?
A place that only your heart can recognize?
   That must be your Tate's Mill.
Take some time!
   Think about it!
      Find it!
What do you want to be?
What do you want to be doing?
How do you want to get there?
It's not hard.
But it does take some time!

Come on in!

I'll meet you here!
Let our journey begin.
Standing on the bluffs at night. Winter. Clear sky. Full
moon. Suddenly this haunting sound comes to you. You
turn and gaze skyward. Geese - wintering here or heading
south? - No matter! The sound is the call of everything wild.
The moonlight reflecting off their wings is the fulfillment of
many dreams.

Just to have seen it -
        is an answer to unspoken prayer.

Now most people would say that today is a miserable sort
of day. Raining pretty heavily. Cool. Temperature in the
50's.

But here in Tate's Mill we take a different look at this. We
got secret places here where -
        you can move in under the rocks, get yourself out
of the wind, out of the rain. You can start a small fire in
front of you. Other people have done this before you. So
this secret place has been secret for a long time. The rock
is worn. When you lean back on it, it's almost like a - like
something that just seems to enfold you. Even though it is
hard, a rock - it welcomes you.

And you can sit in that spot.
You can -

listen to the rain.
And something that a lot of us don't do anymore is just -
listen to the rain.

This isn't a thunderstorm where we've got lightning flashing and thunder rolling all the time. This is just a good, hard rain. And that's all you get to hear is the rain. And the wind.

So -
Take some time.
Listen to it!
Find out what it really says to you.

Listen!   Listen!

One thing about this place that is really great is that it's high up. Almost on the top of the bluff. Not the very top, but close. The view over the rim is - I've always disliked the word "indescribable", but it is the only word that fits. But if I were to try and tell you what this looks like from here, you wouldn't believe me. Nothing I could say would do it justice. The panorama below me is -
You cannot look out here and not see the hand of God.
Awesome God and His handiwork!

It was just me and my dog, Shag that went up here today. At least, that's who we thought it was. We were out for our morning walk and decided to put something special into our day. Work our way into the secret place. Get the fire going' and who comes up beside us but that darn cat. Soaked to the

skin. Looks like it's been beaten and hog tied and dragged.
Looks just plain miserable.

Now you have to understand this. This cat never goes
anywhere. A long trip for her is to the litter box and back
without resting. But she decided this morning to come with
us. But, of course, she neglected to let any of us know. So in
the process, she gets this little extra bath. I tell you, the word
bedraggled describes her exactly at this moment in time.
And today, even the clouds are walking over the rest of the
bluffs. Some people might look at this day and say it's not
a very nice day. It's actually a marvelous, marvelous day.
There aren't many days when you can actually catch the
clouds walking and -
it really looks good. You know? They move slowly over the
bluffs. Like they are guarding the tops of the bluffs.

Not like it's nasty or foreboding or anything else. It's like
a blanket of white that covers them. Kind of an irony that
even when we come to this secret place on dry and sunny
days, we always grab a stick or two. And lay it up. So when
we get days like this, there's no searching involved. We've
got the dry wood we need to start the fire.

And this little place is like a haven. A natural chimney. The
top slopes up so the smoke doesn't sit in here with us. It
tapers down in the back. Got to be a slight breeze coming
in from somewhere, cause it always carries everything out
to the front.
I'm always astounded at things that "seem to work out".
They just don't work out. It's the hand of God in our lives.
And He makes it work out. Things don't just happen!

The cat now has found a spot as close to the fire as she dares. And she is warming and drying herself. She rubbed herself down against - well - against me. And Shag was jealous. But the cat got rid of most of the water. Now she's trying to give the rest to the fire. I wonder how she thinks she is getting back without getting wet again?

I tell you, people that don't have pets are really missing something. There is nothing like watching them. Talking to them. You couldn't ask for better friends. Loyal. Somebody you can always count on. And they don't care what kind of day you've had. Like I've said before, they are going to greet you the same. Everything is okay. All is right in their world! (I carried the cat down inside my jacket).

You can smell the moisture in the air tonight. Lovely. It's that fresh, fresh smell that only comes when the dew is heavy in the air. You know a storm is brewing. You can't see it yet. But you know it's coming. You can smell it!
Not a bad storm.
We're gonna be blessed with a little more rain!
Beautiful times.
Cool. Nice breeze blowing -
        not threatening or anything like that.
Just a night with cool, moist air.

The thing that amazes me about Tate's Mill is this.
        I've lived here my whole life,
                and I'm still being surprised.

I was riding by a cut going back off the ridge. Not a big cut - fairly well wooded. Doesn't go back too far. But, it's one of those things you just kinda tend to overlook. I guess I just happened to turn my head at the right time. "Cause I caught a glint of light off the water.

And this place is -

well, I couldn't see it from the ridge so I rode down into the cut.

Here's this little lake. How deep it is, I don't know. It's one of those you look at it, and you can see the bottom. Little spring running into it from the side. Kinda just hidden from the whole world.

Just sits there.

Peaceful,
Quiet,
Clear,
Beautiful,
Pure.

As I looked around, I could see that this place had been here for who knows how long. And I have been here over 50 years. When we were young, I thought we had crawled over and explored every piece of Tate's Mill and the surrounding area.

But we missed a lot. And this is one of the jewels that we missed. These little surprises in life still make it worthwhile. And bring a smile to your lips.

More than that!

They put a smile in your heart!

These simple little joys that we so quickly tend to overlook and forget about - are still those things that really make us think about who we are.

Another great day for the raptors also. They're on the currents. Just like they are on a merry-go-round that carries them up and down.

THE RIVER

An old bridge.

A challenge more than anything else.

> Half the boards missing - the rest -
> who knows if they'll hold your weight.

And the only thing between you and falling in the river is a little bit of luck. But it's a slow moving river and it runs deep. No one's ever been hurt falling off the bridge. And if they do hit the water, it's only a fall of a couple of feet - but -

it's still the adventure -
> still the chance!

The river has been a witness to so much over its years -

How much does the river know and remember?

> How little it tells!

There is another quiet place. It's called Scarlet Bend. There are a couple of theories on how it was named.

Of course, the old standby - a Woman!

But most people think it's because of the red sand that sits here at this particular point on the river. Creates a little beach. And sitting at the bottom of the bluffs as it does, it's a protected spot. Even though the sun only gets here when it's high in the day,
> if you get here at those times -
>> it's a spot of enormous peace -

and quiet! Quiet so deep it embraces you.
Some place that just lays the warmth and beauty up on you.
A small place of tremendous peace.
No! Not peace - something beyond that!
But what would that word be?

At a small creek today. Two cats down at the creek.

What are they after?

They sat there basking in the warmth of the sun, with only
the song of the brook around us. How long I watched them
- I do not know. Time stood still. And all the time I watched
- neither of those cats moved.

What held them there? What makes them stay silent? And
motionless? Were they simply watching the rest of the
world go by?

Those little streams that feed into the main channel -
Where do they all come from?
Where do they get their water?
I -
have always been amazed by the fact that some of
those streams are always running - and they never dry up.

A couple of times, when I've taken the journey up to the
beginning of some of those streams -

There was one in particular that I had found that
I don't know how to describe it.
This spring came out of the ground -

81

    it was -
I'm sitting here in my mind's eye,
       and I can see it! But how to tell you so you can see
it in the same way!

It just seemed to spring up out of nowhere. And - water
came up -
    with-
            enough force so you can see where it
was coming up -
but there was a pool that had formed here.
 Not a large pool -
Almost like God had put his hand down and pressed in with
His thumb or something and made this little pool here in the
rock. And then leveled out on each side just a little bit - to
give all His creatures purchase from which to drink - when
they came down to the pool.

And away from the spring, the pool just drops away
    deep and clear!
Standing on the edge -
      it looks like you can reach out -
         Touch that pool -
         Touch that bottom.
But I know from experience that you can't. Touch the
bottom, that is. That water is cold and clear and deep. It is
an absolutely marvelous place!
And the only sound you do hear here is -
    the sound of this water.
And it doesn't really
    it doesn't even -

The water doesn't even come up with enough force to break the surface of the water. It kinda just puts a little hump on the surface of the water.

If you're in the pond and you go over there -
>You <u>know</u> that's where the water's coming from.
If someone questions the existence of God, this is the place to take them. No one could imagine this place -
>other than the mind of God!

You can sit here and -
I know the word Eden to me is the image of life and lushness and water the lifeblood of the earth.
And this place puts all that in perspective for you.
Lays it all right out before you.
And all the images will burn in your mind forever. But you are never going to be able to tell anyone adequately how this place is -
>How it looks
>>How it feels
>>>How you felt!
I've come here at every season.
I've come during the lushness of spring -
everything is just bursting with new life
and trying to come up.
I've come here in the summer -
the fullness of growth -
>the greens - so many shades of green you can't even count them.
And the wildlife here is - it's indescribable.

You can sit here for an hour and, if you sit in the perfection of silence, so many things will pass here before you that your heart will stop with the beauty.

With the deer in it's natural element.   The rabbits, pheasants and the prairie chicken. To see these creatures in a place like this - where they have no fear of man. 'Cause no one hunts them here. No harm is done here. All is harmony. It's like this water hole
> this spring
>> this watering of the earth

Is a haven for all.

I've been here in the fall.
> When the colors change. If you think the greens are many -
>> the colors are now in numbers
>>> uncountable.

So many shades of so many colors.
And the rustling as you walk through the leaves as they cover the earth.
> So many sounds!

I've been here in Winter.
In the deep of winter. When the quiet is so heavy, it pulls you into itself. And the only sound you hear - is the sound of silence.

And this protected oasis -
> is a place of quiet! Where the white of Winter seems to hold all sound within itself.

I find myself talking to myself, just to hear

<u>some</u> sound.

But also, I come here for the solitude. For the peace that you find in the solitude here is truly a gift. Known to those who have experienced both loneliness and solitude, and know how to tell the difference.

I've been here in the winter when the snow crunched under each footstep. When it's so cold - you don't want anything exposed.
And the moon is so bright!
And the snow is so white!
Standing here is like standing in a white light.
And you can "hear" how cold it is!

It's so cold this morning that the sun had a hard time coming up!

It's amazing how much of our life is a paradox.
     I hate the cold.
     I hate being cold.
But I love days like this - when it's this cold.
The snow crunches underfoot. Especially when you're out alone. Or with someone you love. (Another paradox)
And the only sound you hear is the sound of your own footsteps.

The skeletons of the trees rustling against each other.

It is always amazing to me how little people really see.
When they look across an expanse -
they don't see anything except blankness and desolation.
These are fields and farms.

And you have the wildlife.
And you have those groves sitting there.

My minds eye picks up the wildlife in there. The rabbit and the wolf and perhaps the bobcat. But most people don't see any of those things. They just see a white, dreary landscape that doesn't seem to have anything going on.

Why can some of us see all of life in the place where they see nothing?

I've been here in the winter when the snow comes in.
And the silence is!
The quiet that you hear - is the sound of silence.
So quiet you can hear your own heart beat.

If the sun catches you right here in the midst of this silence and the warmth beats down on you -

It's like you're sitting on the hand of God.
There's this little community a skip and a jump away from Tate's Mill. It's called Tye's Valley. It's more like a wide cut between the bluffs.

You've never seen a more peaceful town than this.

I happened to walk through it today after the snowfall. It was like walking through a picture postcard.

I've learned that it doesn't do any good to cry about things or complain about it, or anything else. It only does any good if you <u>do</u> something about it.

Are you looking for that place that everybody seems to search for?

Where -
   everything makes perfect sense!

I don't know if such a spot exists. But I do know that here in Tate's Mill, we come awful close.

And while it may not make perfect sense -
Those thing that don't -
   they just seem to fall by the wayside. We take a look at them for what they really are. Most of the time they just don't have any bearing on what is really important in our lives.

And so we just throw those things away here.

And so we can say -
   that most of the time -
     The world here in Tate's Mill

       does make perfect sense!

RIVER RUNNING

There is one group of men that - not just men - one group that for some reason, don't seem like they want to stay. They do! They stay here. And they seem happy.

But when the tugs are running on the river - these folks are standing on the bluffs. And they're watching those tugs and barges move upon the river.

And if you are lucky or unlucky enough to be in a position to see into their eyes, you can see the longing that is there. Those folks who run the river - they don't talk about it - but - kinda like one of those places they've segmented off. The only people they can share it with - is someone who knows where they have been. And even their sharing is strange. 'Cause they'll be two of 'em standing side by side on the bluff - and all they are doing is watching the rig together.

But it's like they've got this "something" that nobody else can get into. Each knows what the other is feeling. No word is said. No contact made other than the presence of a soul mate - who knows and understands exactly what you are feeling. And nothing needs to be said, or indicated, or anything else. That other person just knows - where you are. And he knows the pain you feel in your heart.

He knows the love for the wanderlust -
And he knows the pain! 'Cause he feels it himself and he prays that he is never going to give in to it again.

He has this dream - and somehow - the dream got caught up in reality.

And being the type of person that they are - they take their dreams and set them to the tune of love. And live their life in that reality.

And ever' so often -
you can see them up here on the ridge -
just remembering their dream once more. And they stand there for hours - and watch the river traffic run. We can never know -
what they are going through. 'Cause we've never been there. And most of us will never get there. We never had the courage to run the river. But they did! And now, they feel they have two little advantages on us. They got their memories. - They lived their dream!
Those who have run the river. They can sit on that bluff sometimes for hours.

If you catch their face at just the right angle - there's just the softest smile on their face.
Sometimes,
you can catch the glint of a tear running down their face!
A tear of joy? What memories do they hold inside that can invoke a tear?

I've seen them up there with their wives and girlfriends. And it - it doesn't even change then. They still sit there for hours. The words they exchange you can count on one hand!

And then,
when it's time to leave -
he just gets up

and puts his hand down for their loved one,
And she takes it.
And he pulls her up tenderly,
and holds her like he will fall off the world if she wasn't there.
And they walk away together.

They're both smiling now. And is it because he's made another river run - if only in his mind. She knew him when he was that young man - who made that run. She knows what it's like to miss him. Understands the longing in his heart! Understands also that what holds him here is her -
and his love for her!

What a marvelous relationship those two must have. The depth of feeling! Those are the depths that - most of us will never be able to touch! Would that it were possible!
One young man had run the river for four years. Just one of those - I'm not sure if they consider him lucky or unlucky but he got on the right tug - and had work all year round for four years.
We thought we had lost him forever!

Came back here a changed man. Went away a wild man - willing to do or try anything. Came back a strong man - able to stand anything!
And when you ask him about it,
he just gives you this look that -
I'm not sure if it's the face of an angel - or where it's from -
It's a face where you can see joy - and of such depth that it's without description. Then sadness of such depth it

can break your heart. And images that defy knowledge and take your breath away.

Each of us on every journey takes steps - and sees things that others will never see. And most of the time we never share those things with anyone.

But here in Tate's Mill, sometimes we are able to share those things. If I can see it in his eyes - then he sees it in mine!

SECRET PLACES

Tate's Mill.

Looks like -

Remember those secret places,
    the places where -
        it was just you -
           and maybe your dog?
Nobody else knows about this place!

I had two when I was growing up. One was kinda just on the end of a shelter belt of trees -
    it was an old slough that had been drained and dried. The grass was heavy and thick. Kind of a bit of a hollow. More like a large buffalo wallow. The way the trees were set -
the wind never quite got there. And the way it was set, the sun was always there.
And if you wanted to bake in the sun -
    anytime the sun was shining -
        You could do it in this spot.
You could always find one spot that was protected from the wind. You could just lay there in the sun - and sleep the sleep that cats do in the sun!

The other place was a place I built. It had a southern exposure to it. And we had this rock pile on the north side of this one slough. The slough always had water in it -
    and geese and ducks.
One day I'm looking at this rock pile and this slough -

There was an old wood drag that was lying there also. So I excavated this area, and laid the drag sections across the top and covered it with rock.

I crawled into it. This was a place, too, that caught the sun just about all the time. But the real beauty of this place was that -
> when you were back in here -
the only thing that you could hear was what was directly in front of you.

And what was in front of you was the slough. The ducks or geese out there. You could see them, too. But they never saw you.

People could be standing behind you three feet - they would never know you were there. And you couldn't hear them either.

Marvelous place.

I remember Dad looking for me one day - and when we finally came together, he asked me where I had been. I told him I was out by the slough in the rock pile. And he says,"No. you weren't! I was out there. I was out to the rock pile. I went out there to look for you and you weren't there."
> So - I told him what I had out there.
> And he just looks at me and smiles.
And says that if I was going out there, just to tell him, so he wouldn't have to look. He never came after me when I was

95

in that place. But he wanted to know where I was. And that I was safe. Kind of a shared secret.

But then, Dad was a person who knew the need for secret places.

Then, the other day, the Lord took me to another secret place that I hadn't known before! That I didn't know existed.
But it happened!
It was a cool day and the sun was out.
As I turned to run this one stretch of highway -
      the sun came pouring through the window.
And started to warm me.
All of a sudden, I was at this place where -
      there was -
It is really hard to describe -
It was a peaceful, quiet, feeling that came over me. And I hadn't known peace like that for a long time. We think we do, but we never really do. The warmth that was there at that moment was exactly what I needed. And it's like the Lord knew exactly what I needed at that point in time.

It was just enough to carry me through. Just a small moment in time that made me feel warm, and safe, and comfortable.

These secret places.

What a joy!

What a place - this Tate's Mill!

YOUNG LOVE

And the boys in the boats say they're -

        well, they call it fishing.

They do have fishing poles with them, I guess.
But they're calling to the girls that are on the beaches. And
you can tell which girls they're in love with. Those are the
ones they tease the most.

And evening comes -
And these same boys and girls are together in the streets -
                at the bonfires -
      and-
You wouldn't think that they were even the same people.

The sense of bravado and show -
that they have when their friends are around -
        When it's just the two of 'em.
           All the pretense is gone.

They're not afraid to hold hands -
        and to reach out
            and hold each other.
To share a moment - that no one else can enter into.

Almost like they are in awe
           of what this feeling is.

WONDER

It's the mornings like this that make life really worth living! I wonder how many people really look at it that way? Last night a big snow storm. Everything is covered in a blanket of white.

Everyone's digging out. But still a lot of friendly waves.

These are the times to get into the woods and really experience the quiet. This kind of snow in the woods
the quiet is so deep -
It will reach into your soul.
The kind of quiet -
It's like the Lord reaching in and speaking to your soul. Telling you to look around!
Be quiet! Listen! -
- Listen to the quiet!
And in the same woods -
these ribbons that are streams.
Almost like they are not a part of the wood. A black ribbon of life that flows through it. You can hear the whisper of the water over the rocks.

It's a different sound from the spring and summer time of the running of the water. At this time of year, it's a quiet running.
Almost like it,
while not dormant,
is in a restful state.
And isn't it a wonder -
that we -
are even given the chance to see this-
and hear this.

This Tate's Mill.

C'mon home!

About The Author

Except for a six-year stint in the Marine Corps, the author has lived all of his life in Minnesota. The northwest, in the heart of the Red River Valley, during his growing up years. The Metro with its hustle and bustle, the north central with its lakes and slower paces, the southeast with the bluff country during his working years. He has come to appreciate the differences that are thrust upon us and to enjoy them. He journals these thoughts. Exposed to the corporate fast track he has learned that there are other tracks that we can follow. Most importantly, he has learned that the track that we follow and the pace that we set are of our own choosing.

Printed in the United States
23744LVS00001B/19-45

9 781418 402808